THE DOORWAY TO YOUR SUCCESS

5 Keys to Unlocking Your Door

DEMOINE KINNEY

THE DOOR WAY TO YOUR SUCCESS

Copyright

ISBN: 978-1-943409-70-9
Printed in the United States of America.

Pure Thoughts Publishing, LLC

Demoine Kinney

THE DOOR WAY TO YOUR SUCCESS

Table of Contents

DO YOU KNOW WHO YOU ARE? 5

BE HONEST ABOUT WHAT YOU WANT..................... 15

STOP THE NEGATIVE SELF TALK.................... 28

PLAN FOR YOUR FUTURE SUCCESS 37

TAKE MASSIVE ACTION STEPS.................................. 53

See Your Future Success.. 66

Demoine Kinney

DO YOU KNOW WHO YOU ARE?
KEY #1

I know what you are thinking! This guy can't be serious! Heck yeah I know who I am but my question to you is; do you truly know who you are??? Most people just like me thought we knew who were but had no idea whatsoever. Yes it's very unfortunate but it's true for so many people and part of it is not your fault and part of it is.

What I have discovered is most people identify themselves with who their family wanted them to become, who they thought they should be like or they let situations and circumstances dictate who they are. None of these three things can really show you who you are. In my years of self-discovery I had to learn that it's not what happens to you that make you who you are but how you make it through that shows you who you are.

Do you know that you are a lot stronger than you give yourself credit for? Do you know you are a lot wiser than you give yourself credit for? Do you realize you can change the world based on who you are because you're a change agent? No matter what happens in life, change happens because you are present whether that is positive or negative change, change takes place.

This is something I discovered while serving in the US Air Force. I was supervising a few airmen that were brand new to the Air Force and they all came in with positive attitudes except for one of them. He was always telling me how he didn't like being in the military and how he wanted to do something else.

His attitude was so negative that he changed everybody's temperature everywhere he went because you would be so hot when he left. So many people wanted to fight him it was ridiculous but one day I had an opportunity to talk to him one on one and I asked him "Why do you come off as being so negative?"

He replied "This wasn't my choice to do this; my dad wanted me to join the Air Force because this was his dream but my dream was to go to college."
In that moment I realized "Wow this isn't what he wants!" I didn't know what to say but I asked him "What did you want to go to college to major in?" He replied "I wanted to major in Geology but my dad didn't think I could get a job with that Degree."

My heart truly went out to him because I saw how hurt he was that his dream didn't matter to his dad. I could also tell no matter what he wanted to please his dad. The danger in that though is he may never truly discover who he is if he continues to live out his father's

Demoine Kinney

dreams. The question I also asked was whose to say his father's dreams would have turned out to be great and not a nightmare?

Living out other people's dreams no matter who's they are will not lead you to success or to happiness but living out the ones you see from within will. This leads me to my next point You Have Greatness within you! I know I don't know you personally and you don't know me but I know you were born with your Greatness.

You were placed on Earth to be a **Change Agent** and to bring something different than what the world has ever seen. You don't believe me? Well check this out if you weren't great then why did you make it out of 500 million sperm to your mom's egg and come to the earth? You brought change with you and you brought greatness with you as well.

My favorite book says the race is not given to the swift neither to the strong but those that can endure until the end and guess what!!! That's you! While all those sperm were racing to get to the egg you may not have been the fastest and you made not have been the strongest but you made it to the end and met the egg.

Now let me tell you this I can see the greatness in you all day but you have to now see it within yourself. I know this seems harder than it really is so let me break it down. Take a moment and look back at all of the hard times, difficult moments and hurdles you had to jump over and overcome. Do you see a weak person or an overcomer?

Most of us don't know how to see ourselves, our dreams or our goals because we allow so many people to tell us what they think we should dream and become but if you take a moment you'll realize that makes no sense. If you don't know what I mean listen people say

"You should dream this way or that way in order to become just like XYZ!"

After you hear this type of statement what's the first thing you usually will do? That's right you'll usually start to disregard what you have been seeing within yourself and try to see what the person talking wants you to see. It takes much more work trying to see and imagine what they want than what has naturally been given to you.

I know this is true because I have been there. I was told by a supervisor that it made no sense for me to go to school to get a degree in psychology because there was no money in the industry. He also told me "You should get a degree in IT because there's a lot of money in that." I instantly felt bad for making my own decision to pursue a degree in psychology.

I battled with the idea of switching my degree plan for about 2 weeks and caved to the pressure that I was feeling. I switched my degree to Information Technology Management and left behind my true desire. I know what you're thinking "Why Would you do that?" Well its simple the world we live in today focuses more on money than helping people.

When in all actuality when you take care of people money follows. I remember one of my heroes Bishop TD Jakes saying "Money follows service and it follows passion." I also heard Rita Davenport say some people say "money isn't everything but it ranks right up there with oxygen." Many people think this way and that's what drives them.

I always say don't do what you do for the money but do it for the dream that is within you and money will show up. If money is the only motivator for you then it can lead to a dangerous path that can land you in places you might not want to be. Let your Dream,

Drive and Determination steer you to the path of least resistance.

There's a saying I love "Where focus goes energy flows and results show." So in order to get to the results you see in your dreams you have to focus energy towards that and not allow anyone or anything to stall or even stop you. Just imagine a world where everyone is focused on their dream of becoming great do you have any idea how amazing that would be?

Now that you've finished this chapter I want to ask you a few questions to assist you with your process of unlocking the doorway to your success. These questions are meant to make you think and feel a little uncomfortable so don't worry because they'll change your life.

1) What have you been dreaming about since you were a child and never explored it deeper? The Dreams that

seemed so farfetched that they made your body tingle

_____

_____

_____

_____

_____

_____

_____

_____

_____

2) Why have you not explored those dreams deeper? Who made you feel like those dreams didn't matter?

_____

_____

_____

_____

_____

_____

_____

13

3) What's stopping you from pursuing those dreams now?

_____

_____

_____

_____

_____

_____

BE HONEST ABOUT WHAT YOU WANT
KEY #2

The objective of this chapter is to give you information that will assist you in realizing what being honest with yourself can do in pursuit of your dream life. Also the goal is to show you how to allow yourself the freedom to discover the true essence of who you are through your dreams and raise yourself awareness through affirmations.

Being honest about what you want can seem really simple until it's time to answer the questions to yourself for yourself. I would be lying if I told you I didn't struggle with the very same questions because I did. Most of my life I thought life was all about what other people said I could have and not about what I really wanted.

I allowed myself to be subjected to the will of other people's desires, want and needs by overlooking my own. I'm guessing if you are reading this book right

Demoine Kinney

now you were either the same way or you are that way right now but Guess what??? There's hope for you because I'm going to show you how to stop lying to yourself, get unstuck and help you move forward the life you really want.

In the previous chapter you saw the stories I showed you and probably thought "WOW it's sad how the young man and Demoine disregarded what they really wanted and were unhappy" right? Let me tell you yes it is sad and not for the reasons you might think. It's not about changing the degree or joining the Air Force against a persons will. It's really about the story you tell yourself.

If you tell yourself that other people's feeling are more important than yours then that's how you will react to people's judgement and criticism. If you tell yourself the story that what other people want me to do is more important than what I want for myself then as soon as someone tells you what they think you should do then you'll do that.

You have to learn to first be honest with yourself about what you really want and it seems harder than it is. Remember no one else can see what's inside your head which means no one can see your true dreams and desires but you can. It's so sad how we allow outside forces to tell us what they think is inside of us but we never stand up and say "That's not what I see in my dreams."

You may be saying "Demoine it's not that easy!" I beg to differ because if you think about it how can one see inside of another when it's never truly seen within itself? Example I can't look for greatness in you if I don't see it in myself but I can find flaws in you if that's all I see within myself. People can only judge based on what they see within themselves and nothing more.

Check this out a few years ago I was watching the news and a few children were reported to have been bullied via the internet. Now a lot of adults instantly began to reflect on their childhood and made statements like "People need to stop bullying others on the internet." What they all failed to realize is there is no such thing as cyber bullying because all that needs to be done is the computer need to be turned off.

Anything that can be turned off which one click or touch of a button has no power. The difference in being bullied face to face versus online is the person standing in front of you can't be turned off like a computer and their words can be heard whether you like it or not. Now what you do with those words mean everything so choose wisely what you do with them.

The reality is peoples words only hurt if you believe in your subconscious mind what they are saying. Have you ever heard this saying? "You don't get in life what you think about but you get in life what you are?" This saying is very true because if you walk around in a defeated and negative state you will start to attract that to you.

If you walk around in a low self-esteem state of mind you will attract people who will help you keep your esteem low. You have to make a conscious effort to have high self-esteem because now one can help you with your esteem but you. Hint Hint "SELF ESTEEM" Now like I said before don't get down on yourself about the way you have been I'm going to show you how to turn things around.

Now there's a powerful tool I use all the time that changed my life and I'm going to teach it to you right now. Are You Ready? Here it goes! You have to start Affirming Yourself! Self-Affirmation is something we all must do every day because no one can do that for you. This process helps you make up your mind on who you are and want to become.

I write affirmations often to remind myself of how powerful, strong, smart, ambitious, loving, kind, and focused I am. Now the key to affirm yourself with all positive things because you already have had enough negative affirmations in your life. Did you know it takes sixteen positive messages to drown out one negative message?

Many people don't know this and that can be the very thing to keep people hung up on things that hurt them. Just imagine if you waited on people every day to tell you who you are, how beautiful you are, how smart you are or even to tell you how much value you add to the lives of other people. What I know about you is you have the power to change not only the world but your own life!

Think about this for a moment do you think a police officer or fire fighter is thanked every day for doing what they do? Do you think they wait on people to confirm that they are a police officer or fire fighter before they show up to work? Do you think they stand in the mirror in the morning and wish someone would appear and say go be a cop or firefighter today?

Just like me I'm sure you know the answers to those questions are of course not they just go and be who they are and do what they do. Nobody should have to appear in your mirror either but to tell you all of the things you need to hear and things that you already know subconsciously about yourself. This is my personal belief nobody should treat me better than I treat myself and I shouldn't take care of people better than I take care of myself.

There is another quote I love and you can borrow this one "Do unto yourself as you would do unto others." Great one right? Now you may be thinking that's the total opposite of what you have been used to hearing. We are taught Do unto others as you would do unto you and that's great but sometimes you see Greatness in other people and you tell them but want do that for yourself.

I know you may be thinking at this point in the chapter so you mean to tell me I have been thinking wrong about myself? The answer is Yes! I'm here to tell you and coach you in through your process of self-discovery. You have to start complimenting yourself just as much as you compliment other people that way you hold the power and not someone else.

Ok think about this when human being look for a mate you typically end up finding someone who reminds you of your mom, dad, siblings, grandparents and so on and so forth but what's wrong with finding someone who reminds you of yourself? There is absolutely nothing wrong with thinking and affirming that you want someone who reminds you of you.

Look at this for a moment if you read my favorite book it says there was a man who was in a garden alone and one day his creator said he shouldn't be alone. So the man was put to sleep and a rib was removed and a woman was created. This is a powerful story if you really see what's happening here. The man was given back to him what was in him the entire time.

There were was no hammers, saws, wood, metal or glass used but the thing that was inside the man the entire time was used to bless him. If you take the man out of the equation and put yourself there you'll see that what is made to bless you is already inside of you. There is nothing from without/around you that can bless you the way the things that are within you can.

Before I close out this chapter I want you to see this African Proverb that I read often "When there is no enemy within, the enemy outside can do you no harm. As you see the enemy outside of you can do nothing to you but the enemy within yourself can change everything. Are you your own worst enemy?

The objective of this chapter was to give you information that will assist you in realizing what being honest with yourself can do in pursuit of your dream life. Also the goal was to show you how to allow yourself the freedom to discover the true essence of who you are through your dreams and raise yourself awareness through affirmations.

Now that you've finished this chapter I want to ask you a few questions to assist you with your process of unlocking the doorway to your success. These questions are meant to make you think and feel a little uncomfortable so don't worry because they'll change your life.

I have so much more I have to share with you but before I do though I want you to think about and answer the following questions.

1) What dreams and visions are trapped inside of you that you haven't allowed to be exposed yet?

_____

_____

_____

_____

_____

_____

_____

_____

2) What things have you told yourself that are not true?

_____

_____

_____

_____

_____

_____

3) Why are you denying yourself the opportunity to be great?

_____

_____

_____

_____

_____

_____

_____

_____

Demoine Kinney

These dreams you listed are important because no one that you see on a daily basis gave you those dreams. You were born with them and they came to you naturally. You had absolutely nothing to do with those dreams but they are yours now. I'm going to tell you a secret that you already know! You are the owner of those dreams and they can't be birthed out through anyone else but you.

No one can get inside your head or your dreams and see what you saw. One thing I know about you is you are a creative genius and your dreams can come true and they will come true but not until you make the decision to do a few things that I'm going to teach and share with you.

1) Write down your most vivid dreams (Day dreams or night dreams)
2) Speak to those dreams as if you are living in the moments now. (Affirmations)
3) Practice what you saw in those dreams daily
4) Live out those dreams daily.

Demoine Kinney

"One of the greatest tragedies in life is to watch potential die untapped."

-Myles Munroe-

STOP THE NEGATIVE SELF TALK

Key #3

The objective for this chapter is to assist you with recognizing what you say to yourself and what you receive from other people in conversations. Also it is to help you to correct the inner conversations you have with yourself and give you a few tools to help you to propel to the next level of your life.

This Key is a very important one because we all have a habit of talking ourselves out of things before we even begin the process. I was asked a question recently which was "Demoine hug your wife." I reached towards my wife and hugged her then I was asked to try to hug my wife and I reached again. It was said no I didn't say do it I said Try to do it.

The funny thing about it is I had been instructed to do this before by my coach Lisa Nichols and I got the same answer. When you try nothing happens but when you do something then it happens. Everything we try to do is stuck in our minds and we exhaust our energy in our minds before our body can even attempt to perform the action asked.

You may be wondering what that is that stops you and I'm going to answer it for you now. It's called negative self-talk. Negative self-talk is the very thing that stops a lot of us from even attempting to do a thing. For instance if I know I want to go to college and I tell myself "I could never make it in college." Guess what I won't!

If I tell myself "I really would love to be married one day but I could never be a good husband", you won't! Some of us are stuck in a rut right now because of the things that you say to yourself. The crazy thing is more of us do it than not. Ask yourself this question when was the last time I told myself I can't do something? For some it may be this morning or for some 5 minutes ago.

I personally was stuck in this rut myself for a number of years. When I was serving in the Air Force I made myself believe that I couldn't make E6 the first time I tested for it. Now the odds stacked against me but not so high that it wasn't attainable. I knew people who had made the rank the first time through but because of what everyone else said I drunk the Kool-Aid.

I began my studies for the promotion 3 months before the test date, prepared my study area at home to give myself the right environment and I also bought every resource possible to make it possible to score just what I needed to make the rank. Now what I also brought was a conversation that may sound familiar to you "Man I'm going to study but if I don't make it, it's all good. At least I tried!"

You have probably said the exact same thing to yourself when preparing for a test too. Day after day I brought that same attitude into my study environment. After months of studying it was now the day for me to test for E6. As I walked into the room my hands began to sweat, my legs became numb and my chest began to tighten.

Just as I took my seat the test proctor exclaimed "Sir you didn't sign in!" I forced myself out of my seat and began the long cold walk to her sign in sheet which was sitting on her desk in the front of the room. After signing my name I returned to my seat and began to pray. "Lord you know and I know that I studied so I'm just asking you to let me recognize this stuff on this test. Please Sweet baby Jesus!"

About 3 minutes later I heard the words thought I was prepared for but dreaded at the same time "The Test Starts Now!" I immediately felt myself go numb and nervous at the same time. I answered the first question reluctantly and thought to myself "well here's we go." After getting to approximately question 50 I began thinking "just do your best Demoine but if you don't make it you have next year."

As I came down the home stretch I felt myself settling down and I said to myself one more time "Just do your best Demoine but if you don't make it you have next year." Shortly after finishing the sentence I answered the last question and leaped out of my seat to turn in the answer sheet and booklet. I was so relieved to be finished with the test.

3 months passed by and it was day to get the results and I was so nervous. One of my friends was on his computer checking to see if his name was on the list of promotes and he looked nervous but excited as

well. As he scrolled and looked for his name I thought to myself "Don't worry Demoine it's all good because you studied but if you don't make it you have next year."

My friend finally got to his last name and to his surprise he did not make E6 but had missed it by .96 points. He kept scrolling until he got to the K's and looked for my name. As he scrolled I felt like I couldn't swallow at all. He got closer to my name and said "Dang bro you missed it by 1 point!" There I was sitting there in shock and dismay.

At that moment I was disappointed in myself not because I didn't study but because I felt I had set myself up for failure. I kept thinking about how many times I told myself "just do your best Demoine but if you don't make it you have next year." I felt like I should have never told myself that but I should have told myself "Demoine You can and You Will Make it no matter what!"

That is a moment I will never forget in life because it helped shape my new thought process. I'm not saying I'm perfect at it yet but what I am saying is

32

that I make a conscious effort to tell myself I can and I will now. I honestly believe that if we to tell our self what we can and will do then we have a huge chance of making things happen.

I think back now and say to myself "I shouldn't have made the next year an option in my mind because I knew it was possible for me to make E6 my first year. It's amazing how much control we really do have when it comes to outcomes in life. Many of us talk ourselves out of great things, opportunities and situations because of what we say to ourselves.

One thing I noticed too which I have to point out is that a lot of us say "They said" Who is they?? If you talk to people who often say "they Said" ask them who are they that said whatever was said? You'll be surprised with the answer you receive. Most people hear themselves talking when they are afraid to take a major step in life and they think other people are talking to them.

I used to be the same way and I really believed that there were people telling me what I could and couldn't do but the reality was I was telling myself that I couldn't do things. I want you to know that your dreams are so big that they can scare you but what you need to know is that you have to pursue your dreams scared! Don't let fear stop you but let it be fuel that will drive you to success.

My favorite book says we don't have a spirit of fear but of love and of a sound mind. Which simply means that my spirit knows no fear and the love that is within me will allow me to still make sound decisions in life. You have to make a sound decision to pursue your dreams and let nothing or no one stop you from obtaining and attaining what is already yours. It's your birth right.

The objective for this chapter was to assist you with recognizing what you say to yourself and what you receive from other people in conversations. Also it was to help you to correct the inner conversations you have with yourself and give you a few tools to help you to propel to the next level of your life.

Now that you've finished this chapter I want to ask you a few questions to assist you with your process of unlocking the doorway to your success. These questions are meant to make you think and feel a little uncomfortable so don't worry because they'll change your life.

I have so much more I have to share with you but before I do though I want you to think about and answer the following questions.

1) What negative self-talk have you been having with yourself?

_____

_____

_____

_____

_____

_____

_____

_____

2) Name 3 times where you talked yourself out of doing what your heart truly desired.

_____
_____
_____
_____
_____
_____
_____
_____

3) List 3 Affirmation you know you need to start saying to yourself every day?

i.e. I am the architect of my life; I build its foundation and choose its Contents.

_____
_____
_____
_____
_____
_____
_____
_____

PLAN FOR YOUR FUTURE SUCCESS
KEY #4

In this chapter the objective is to teach you how to plan for your future, show you what not planning can delay your future and to give you the necessary tools to plan effectively. The goal is to grant you access to another key to the doorway of your success.

I grew up in a small town called Dillon SC and while in high school I was in the marching band. I had an instructor who I still talk to today and consider a friend Mr. Adrian Wright who used to have a lot of sayings that I still remember. Now there are a few that stuck with me more than others so I'm going to share them with you right now. One of his saying was "if you fail to plan then you plan to fail."

Another one was "To be on time is to be late and to be on time is to be early" and the last one is "piss poor effort get you piss poor performance." No I hope that you didn't and don't get offended by the

Demoine Kinney

wording but actually look at what he was saying. What I learned from him is you can't just do whatever and expect greatness.

These were words I needed to hear growing up because I was a young guy who was being raised without a father because my dad died when I was 6. Now my Grandfather and my Uncles played a major part in my upbringing and they had sayings to but to not bore you I'll stick with Mr. Wright's sayings. Even though most of us in high school didn't want to hear the saying they were life changing.

Now let's look at these sayings one by one and break them down. The first one I shared was "If you fail to plan then you fail to plan." The question I have for you is what is life without a plan? Are you thinking? Let me help you "It's a mess!" I have met many people from all walks of life who have told me "I'm a go with the flow type of person.

You know what that really means? It means I don't like to have structure in my life so as an excuse for any failures or mistakes I just go with the flow of whatever happens. Planning doesn't only provide structure but accountability in your life. I don't know about you but I personally need the structure and accountability in my life because it helps to guide my days, my weeks, my months and my years.

My favorite books says people perish due to a lack of knowledge and know it has many meanings to many people but I believe if you lack the knowledge of your purpose, passion and plan you will perish. I believe this because I see many people wasting their life away and their excuse is nobody taught me or nobody showed me. The key is knowing what you want and finding the people to help you.

Nobody is coming to your house to show you anything but you can plan to go to seminars, workshops and other places where the people are that are doing what you feel is your purpose and passion as well. I remember learning how to place the sax at the age of 12 no one was there to teach me

THE DOOR WAY TO YOUR SUCCESS

because the one person I trusted to teach me died the same day I got my saxophone Mr. Larry Johnson.

How I met Mr. Johnson though was one day he came to my school cafeteria called Gordon elementary school with a group of students and he had all of the students demonstrate the sound of every instrument. As soon as I heard the saxophone I knew that was the instrument I wanted to learn how to play. As soon as the demonstration was over I ran to the front of the room and asked for the brochure.

I was so excited to take the brochure home to my mom to show her what I wanted to play. Later that day the bus pulled up to my house and I jumped out of my seat and ran in the house to show my mom this amazing instrument I wanted to learn more about. When I got in the house I pulled the brochure out and said "Mom Mom! I want one of these I want to learn how to play it."

My mom looked at me and said "Ok we'll have to get the money for it if you really want to learn how to play it." Instantly I replied "Ma I'll do whatever it takes to get one!" A few weeks prior to meeting Mr. Johnson and the students from the demonstration my teaching Mr. Moody offered the students an opportunity to work during the summer so I made it up in my mind "I'm gonna work for Mr. Moody."

When I returned to school that Monday I walked up to Mr. Moody and asked "Mr. Moody can I work for you this summer? I have something I'm trying to buy." He told me yes and said all you have to do is have your mom call me and I'll let you work with me.

That summer I promised myself no matter what happens I'm going to get myself a Saxophone and I'll work with Mr. Moody, My Granddad or whoever else I needed to work with in order to make the money. I was willing to do everything but sell drugs to get it though so let's get that straight right now. LOL!! Besides how would it look for me to sell drugs while playing a saxophone what would I do sell from the bell of my horn? LOL!!

Anyway, I worked the entire summer to make the $1200 needed to get my saxophone and you know what!! I got it! The funny thing though was as soon as I had enough money my mom went and got the Saxophone and told me to keep the money I had made. You know what I did! I laid that money across the bed and played the Sax to it every day for about 3 months. LOL!!

My point of sharing this story is to show you that I had a plan to get what I wanted at the age of 12. Just imagine if you did the same thing at the age you are right now. Guess what though! It's possible. Say this with me now "It is Possible". I want you to know that it is possible for you to live your dreams, it is possible for you to be successful and it is possible for you to live in your Greatness!

You can have everything that you dream! I know you've been told the opposite but I'm not here to lie to you but I'm here to tell you that truth "Your Dreams are your and whatever you Dream is meant for you to pursue." Your dreams are not selfish but they serve a purpose and most likely they'll have you in a space where you are serving others.

Now that you are on your path to opening up the doorway let me share a few effective things that I

42

have also used to help me open the door to my success. I am a student of World Famous Speaker, Author and Coach Tony Robins and he uses a method called "The Rapid Planning Method" which changed my life forever. This method is not about managing time but it's a system of thinking.

Most people think that planning is all about managing time but it's not it's truly about managing your life and things that keep you fulfilled. There a few questions you have to always ask yourself

1) What results do I want to see in my life?

2) What is my purpose?

3) What am I willing to do to make it happen?

In life we need a plan in order to set the stage for what we say we really want. Most of us focused so much on what we didn't want that we started attracting that. For instance I came from a family where a lot of men slept with multiple women cheated on their wives and were abusive and my goal was to not be like that. So when I was afraid to

43

get married because I didn't want to make those mistakes.

Just before I met my wife Marita Kinney I found out there were things I could do to refocus my mind not on what I didn't want but what I truly wanted and desired. Now Marita and I have been married over 8 years and my mind is only focused on being the best husband I can be. In life you get what you focus on whether that be good or bad.

I encourage you today to make a conscious choice today to focus only on what you want and not what you don't want in life. You owe it to yourself to reach your full potential because remember no one else can birth out the things you were placed here on Earth to birth out. No one can live out your dreams for you and no one can do your pushups for you.

Which leads me to my next point Mr. Wright had 2 more saying that have changed things for me in life and they are "To be on time is to be late and to be on time is to be early" and "piss poor effort get you piss poor performance." I want you to really look at this and realize that this is not only true but it's vital to your everyday life.

For instance if you are late to everything in life you could miss a great opportunity that could be the very thing you have been praying for and waiting to see. You must plan to always be early so that you show up on time which simply means be proactive and not reactive to situations. When you're late you feel stress and worry because you don't know what you missed or will be missing.

In the military we are taught to always be at least 15 minutes early to your appointments but I know people who go to an appointment and see that is says on the wall "We will still take you as long as you're not 10 mins past your appointment time. I personally never wanted to test the limits on things like that because I believed if I true that statement I will start a terrible habit of it.

Now I understand things happen but there is no reason why anyone should be late to everything. It shows you can't be trusted and it also shows that you are not consistent. If you show up to work late everyday eventually you will be known as the unreliable person and you will be terminated. Being on time isn't just for you but for those who may be depending on you as well.

So the last point I want you to share with you is about performance. I heard a saying from Mr. Les Brown that says "Anything that is worth doing is worth doing badly." This is true on so many levels but you should always strive to get better at whatever you feel is worth doing. You cannot perform the same way you did on something you have been doing for 10 years like you did the day you started.

Everything you do should be done on a level that lets yourself and others know that you mean business and that you are doing what you love. You may be asking "What does this have to do with planning my future success?", and I'm here to show you. Whatever you believe is for you to do it requires a plan. There has to be a road map that guides you to whatever your desired outcome is.

I personally plan things in my life so I won't become easily distracted with other things. Like the time my wife and I moved to a new house I knew there were things we wanted to update in and outside the house. I knew if I didn't plan for each project I was going to spend too much money, time and effort and possibly see no progress but chaos.

Have you ever done that before? You start cleaning your house and there are 4 rooms that need your attention so you do a little bit in each room and before you realize it you're exhausted and you look in each of the rooms and it seems like you have gotten nowhere. O yes I know the feeling and it sucks! I learned to plan out each project and stick to the plan until it's finished.

That's exactly what you have to do in your life when it comes to pursuing those dreams that you have. You have to write the dreams down, create a road map and set a solid plan that will allow you to start moving forward until you reach the destination. I'm sure you do the same thing when you're traveling on a road trip or at least I hope so.

I don't know too many people that just jump in a car and drive 5 hours if you haven't checked the best route, the timing it will take to get there, see if you enough gas to get there or had a place in mind that you were even going. If you wouldn't do that in a

47

car why do we do this in our life? It's amazing how the greatest secrets to success in life are being revealed every day.

Before I close out this chapter I want to share one of my most powerful tools that you can use to get you to where you want to go as well. It's called!!! Are You Ready??? "A VISON BOARD" Any dreams and visions that you have should be placed on your vision board because this is a tool that you can look at every day. Each year my family and I do vision boards because we all have goals, dreams and visions and we want to have a clear picture of what we have seen inside.

Isn't it funny that you can hear something and forget it within minutes but when you write it down it's hard to forget what you wrote? Especially if you keep it in a place that you have to go everyday like your bathroom, bedroom, your car and etc. The good thing about having a vision board too is as you see the things that are on you board come true in your life now you feel a sense of accomplishment.

So now that you have this tool you can start right now with your vision board and use it to assist with your journey. Always remember this success leaves clues but you have to know where to look. Don't over think things because that's what makes it complicated but everything you need is inside of you. No dream is too big or too small so get your vision board started now.

In this chapter the objective was to teach you how to plan for your future, show you how not planning can delay your future and to give you the necessary tools to plan effectively. The goal is to grant you access to another key to the doorway of your success.

Now that you've finished this chapter I want to ask you a few questions to assist you with your process of unlocking the doorway to your success. These questions are meant to make you think and feel a little uncomfortable so don't worry because they'll change your life.

I have so much more I have to share with you but before I do though I want you to think about and answer the following questions.

THE DOOR WAY TO YOUR SUCCESS

1) What Goals did you have in the past that you still haven't reached yet?

_____

_____

_____

_____

_____

_____

_____

_____

2) What are you willing to do to start seeing a different outcome?

_____

_____

_____

_____

_____

_____

_____

_____

Demoine Kinney

3) List Your New Goals and list one Action step beside them.

_____

_____

_____

_____

_____

_____

_____

_____

_____

4) What day are you going to start moving towards your goals and why?

_____

_____

_____

_____

_____

_____

_____

Demoine Kinney

"Success is not final; failure is not fatal: It is the courage to continue that counts."

-- Winston S. Churchil

TAKE MASSIVE ACTION STEPS
KEY #5

In this Chapter the objective is to share what I have done to take massive action steps in my life and teach you how you can do the same. The goal is to grant you access to another powerful key to the doorway of your success.

Now let me warn you before we get started this key is so powerful it will cause you to move in a direction you have never gone before. This key causes many people to gracefully bow out and settle for a mediocre life. This key has caused many people to say it's just not worth it but I believe in you and I believe you are ready for this key.

So let's move forward with granting you the access you have been waiting for and you deserve. Throughout the course of my life I have had to make not only a decision to change things but I had to take what I

53

consider to be massive action steps towards the life I truly desire. Many people think that it's all in the decision but I 'm here to let you know it's about the steps also.

When I was growing up in South Carolina we were always in church and I recall hearing the pastor say "The steps of a good man are ordered by the Lord." I believe that is true and I also believe that when we step it must be in order. What I mean is every step you take should be calculated and in faith.

I believe that everything worth having is worth fighting for, planning for, having faith for and also preparing for. Some people think that it's all about faith but that's an out of balance way of thinking. My favorite book says "Faith without work is dead." So this means you can have all the faith you want but some work has to be done too.

For example if I'm at school and my professor gives me all the material needed,

54

gives a lecture and says take notes then tells me we have a test coming up on Friday I have to put in some work to ensure I'm prepared for the test. Now if I never review the notes given or the material I can't expect to pass the test. So you can have a lot of faith but that will not guarantee a passing score.

I know this to be true because it happened to me. There were times when I was pursuing my Bachelor's degree in Information Technology Management when I heard my professor say take notes but I thought to myself "I'll remember it" and I didn't. A few days later I struggled trying to remember everything that was said but I couldn't so on test day I didn't score the highest but I passed.

The point that I passed seemed like it should have been good enough for me but it wasn't because I knew I didn't do all that I could to get the best grade possible. I could have chosen to blame my professor, my fellow

Demoine Kinney

Which leads me to this point in my life. We have been taught that if we take baby steps, then we are ok. I'm here to tell you, that's not true! You should take **Massive Action Steps** in your life every day! I remember hearing one of my coach's talk about taking massive action and I was thinking to myself "What about the baby steps I was always told were good enough."

Massive action steps isn't something that you do one time and expect great results but it's something that you must do time and time again in order to get to the life you truly desire and want. Think about it like this for that know me or have seen me on television I have done multiple live comedy appearances on TV but it didn't happen without taking massive action steps.

As a standup comedian it took me years of writing jokes, trying the jokes at amateur night at various comedy clubs, researching

TV shows that were coming out that would possibly give me an opportunity to audition and quite a few other things. Now if I stayed at home and just wrote a bunch of jokes and never went out to the clubs to try the jokes there's no telling how many opportunities I would have missed.

I want to give you this piece of advice to help you "In life you don't get what you think about you get what you are." If you strive for greatness you get greatness but if you do nothing but think about trying to do something nothing happens. Where ever you place focus and attention your energy will flow in that direction.

So just like I had to keep taking massive action steps to get on TV you have to take continuous massive action steps to reach your goals and obtain your dream life. Now that I have told you about massive action steps let me show you how effective this tool is.

I have attached a diagram below to show you what focused energy can allow you to accomplish with massive action steps being applied. Let's just say you would like to obtain a bachelor's degree in two years and you know all the steps required so now you just need to write them down. Here is what the massive action steps might look like to make this goal a reality.

THE DOOR WAY TO YOUR SUCCESS

Massive Action Step	Result	Purpose
Start researching potential colleges		To have an idea of potential schools and to see the requirements to be accepted
Prepare and take your placement tests (SAT or ACT)		To show your strongest areas of focus
Submit applications to your desired schools	**To Obtain a Bachelor's Degree in 2 years**	To see if you're accepted
Submit Applications for financial aid (FAFSA)		To see if you qualify for grants and scholarships
Once accepted pick a degree plan		To obtain a focus area
Turn in all assignments weekly		To keep yourself accountable and maintain the GPA required to graduate
Take Summer classes		To stay on your 2 year graduation track
Apply For Graduation		To attend your commencement ceremony

Demoine Kinney

As you can see a detailed massive action step plan can lead you to graduating with a bachelor's degree in 2 years but not only that it can lead you to success with any goals you may have in life. You don't have to live a limited life because of limiting beliefs any longer. You can live an abundant life with massive action steps.

Your dreams don't have to stay dreams but they can become your reality every day when you ask yourself the right questions, answer them honestly and write down the massive action steps needed to go as far as your dreams take you. Turning your dreams into reality is as easy as 1-2-3 and you can believe that.

Everything that has been covered so far in this book has given you tools and keys to opening the doorway to your success but I also want to give you a bonus. How would you like that? Would you like to know what the bonus is?

Of course you would! Now your bonus is!!!! Now that you have finished this book and received these secret keys to success you are a part of a very unique tribe of people called "The Gatekeepers of Success!" This is a powerful group of influencers that you are now a part of. This is an awesome thing to obtain not because of the position itself but because of the influence that you now have on yourself and those around you.

You are a change agent now and have the power to invoke change everywhere you go. Never go back to the old ways of thinking but live in your new reality knowing that you truly have the power to make a difference in your local, regional, state, country and worldwide. Nothing in this world can stop you now and that's something you have to be proud of.

In this Chapter the objective was to share what I have done to take massive action steps in my life, how I did it and to teach you how you can do the same. The goal was to grant you access to another powerful key to the doorway of your success.

Now that you've finished this chapter I want to ask you a few questions to assist you with your process of unlocking the doorway to your success. These questions are meant to make you think and feel a little uncomfortable so don't worry because they'll change your life.

I have so much more I have to share with you but before I do though I want you to think about and answer the following questions.

1) List 3 Massive Action steps taking you know you have to take.

_____

_____

_____

_____

_____

_____

_____

_____

_____

2) What is your first Massive Action step going to be towards your success?

_____

_____

_____

_____

_____

_____

_____

_____

_____

3) Why are these Action Steps important to you?

_____

_____

_____

_____

_____

_____

_____

_____

Demoine Kinney

See Your Future Success

By looking at the title of this chapter you may be wondering "What does he mean by See My Future Success". Well I'm glad you're curious to know. Seeing your future success is vital in this process of self-discovery. Most people only see themselves where they are currently and never attempted to take look at where they could be. I have met so many people while traveling with the military and during speaking engagements who come to me with the conversation like "I don't know whether I'm coming or going sometimes". I just smile and say I know what the problem might be and it's simple actually. They ask "Well if you can see the problem can you tell me so I can get it right?" I say "Yes I can tell you that you are not doing life visioning exercises on a daily basis to see where you could be verses seeing where you are right now." Now that I let you in on the common conversation that I have with others let me ask you, how often do you do life visioning exercises? How often do you meditate?

When and if you do for how long do you meditate and do life visioning exercises? These two things are a part of my daily life and my life has been so much better for it. I heard about Life visioning from an amazing Pastor by the name of Michael B. Beckwith who pastors the Agape International Spiritual Center in Beverly Hills, California. He developed the 4 stages of Life Visioning that changed my life and I believe they will change yours as well. The 4 steps are Life is happening to Me, Life is happening to it, By Me, Life is happening Through Me and Life is happening As Me. Basically what the steps illustrate is going from a mentality of victim hood which is step one to become one with the infinite source and recognizing that you are connected with it. Many of us believe there is a separation between us and our creator and that is not true at all. We are connected to our source more than we think. My favorite book says "Then God said "Let us make mankind in our image, in our likeness, so that they may rule over the fish in the sea and the birds in sky, over the livestock and all the wild animals, and over all the creatures that move along the ground."(Genesis

1:26). Every time I read this passage it helps me realize that we are connected with our source and there is no separation because we are one in spirit and we look just like our father. It's amazing how most religious groups are taught that God is sitting up high and looking down low at us not realizing that he is within us. I call the source God and some call it the universe or the source but no matter what you call it we understand the point. It is my belief that we all have been placed here for a purpose and on purpose because no one is here just to take up space and breathe air. I also believe that we are all connected we are all limitless beings and anything that we can envision during our life visioning exercises we can actually become and manifest it in our daily lives. Most people who come to counseling say they aren't sure what they like to do and my response is, "who you are is more important that what you do." Many of us think what we do for a living and in our leisure time is more important than who we are which is very far from the truth. Who you are as a person actually dictates what you do and it shows not only other people but also yourself what values you have and where your interests are. Often when speaking my clients the goal is to have them to think about what they find yourselves doing when no one else is around, also to think for a moment about what their thoughts are about most when they are alone and lastly, to consider when their watching TV what do their tend to watch on a regular basis? These things can help you to determine the type of person you really are. I challenge you to consider the same questions without judgment but to gain more insight about who you are and what your interests are. I often ask the questions in reference to when the client is alone because most of us are people pleasers and we will conform to doing what the crowd wants to do whether we truly enjoy the particular activity and environment or not. What you do when you're alone says a lot about you. I've heard people say I don't like being alone and I know why that could be. We are relational beings and we feed off of the energy of others but I truly believe that we must get to know ourselves first. Knowing yourself, your values and your own interests are important not only while for relationships but for your quality of life. You are here on Earth to make an impact and enjoy your quality of life while you're here. While reading a book entitled "The 7 Habits of Highly Effective People" written by Stephen Covey, he states "We must begin with the end in mind". This means when we think about our lives we must think about our end/our funeral and what we want people to say about us. We must understand that every day we live it should be prioritized based on how effective we want to be and not how many things we want to do. I know you may be wondering what does all of this have to do with Life Visioning and that is a great question. It has everything to do with what I'm bringing to your attention. When you begin and end your day with Life Visioning it allows you to gain insight on the things that are most important, it allows you to hear from the source at the beginning and ending of your day and it also helps you to celebrate the successes of the day instead of just letting them pass you by like the wind. I practice Life Visioning daily to help me begin my day grounded and centered so that I am positioned to be effective and not just busy. Many of us spend more time being busy and less effective because we have bought into the idea that the more activities you do in a day makes you more of a BOSS than someone else. When in all actuality just like Tyler Perry has stated many times "If you have a one bucket of water and you plant seven seeds in the ground you will not be able to water all of the seeds enough for them all to grow. You must focus on one seed at a time and then move on to the next one and allow it to grow as well." For some this can be a challenge because in today's world we all suffer from information overload from TV and social media. Everywhere you turn there are advertisements and people talking about quitting your job to pursue your passions. They also say you can have more than what you have right now but I truly believe that having more stuff doesn't make you happy but it will require more of your time to maintain all that you have. This is another reason why I practice life visioning because it helps you to see what is more important. While doing life visioning I can honestly tell you that I've never seen myself with a whole lot of stuff but I typically see myself helping others, starting initiatives, traveling with my family and doing things that actually help others. I would encourage you begin your process of life visioning today and watch your life change. All it takes is for you to close sit in a chair with your back straight, close your eyes, place your feet flat on the floor, place your hands on your knees in a relaxed position and you will need to take a 3 breathes in and out. When breathing you want to take in air for 6 counts and breathe out for 3. You should be able to hear your heartbeat at this time and you want to embrace that moment. Learn to appreciate your heartbeat and learn to appreciate the air you breathe. Clear your mind by saying let go and relax your entire body as if you are going limp. Once you do this just allow images to appear in your mind and pay attention to what you see. After about 10 mins of this write down what you saw and place it on your vision board. Once you have done this for about a week you can increase your time in meditation and trust me when I tell you life will becoming more clear to you. You will now begin to See Your Future Success clearly.

You have reached the end of this powerful book but I want you to know something "You're on your way to living the life of your dreams and unlocking the doorway to your success." Your dreams are yours so own them and never forget that only you can birth out what's inside of you and you can never be robbed of your true dreams.

No burglar can break into your head and steal your dreams and no one can make you believe that your dreams aren't real. Live your best life now because you never know when your last day will be. You owe it to yourself and the world to bring the change that only you can. So today is your resurrection day!

My favorite book says "no eyes have seen and no ear has heard neither has entered into the heart of man the things that God has prepared for them that love him." And lastly I want to have faith and believe that your dreams matter and that they have meaning I want to leave you with this Faith comes by hearing and hearing so what do you hear?

Pay attention to who and what you listen to because it can either push you to your greatness or distract you from getting to your greatness. No matter what happens in life you have to know that the greatness that you have inside of you is yours and it's your birthright.

I pray for your success, your vision, your hearing, your eyesight and your mindsight. Know that I'm in your corner cheering you on and I hope to see you soon at one of my seminars so stay tuned by going to www.demoinekinney.com or you can follow me on social media on Facebook, Instagram and Twitter by typing in my name Demoine Kinney.

I look forward to hearing from you soon.

God bless You my friend,
Demoine Kinney

-Your success is not dictated by anyone but you-
Demoine Kinney

ABOUT AUTHOR

Dr. A. Demoine Kinney is one of the world's most-requested life purpose coaches, trainers and transformational speakers, as well as comedian, media personality and corporate CEO whose global platform has reached and served nearly 30 million people. From a struggling disabled veteran with PTSD to a millionaire entrepreneur, Demoine's courage and determination has inspired fans worldwide and helped countless audience's breakthrough, to discover their own untapped talents and infinite potential. As Founder and Chief Executive Officer of Eksadas Entertainment Group LLC., Warriors Operation Healing Inc. and The Kids Acting Academy Inc. one of the Atlanta, Georgia's most sought out film and television production as well as personal and business development training and Kids/Teen Performing Arts companies – Dr. Kinney has helped develop workshops and programs that have transformed the lives of Kids, Teens, men and women, and has altered the trajectory of individuals and businesses throughout the country and across the world.

Dr. Kinney is also a best-selling author of 5 books, and his 5th book Manhood: The Struggles of a Man, published by Pure Thoughts Publishing. In Manhood: The Struggles of a Man, Dr. Kinney continues his with his fans, providing a clear and practical blueprint for personal success, drawn directly from the life experiences of its beloved author. Manhood: The Struggles of a Man is the follow-up to Dr. Kinney Amazon's bestseller, When His Joy Falls.